Jackie Robinson

Hero on the Baseball Field

Stephanie E. Macceca

Consultant

Glenn Manns, M.A.
Teaching American History Coordinator
Ohio Valley Educational Cooperative

Publishing Credits

Dona Herweck Rice, *Editor-in-Chief*; Lee Aucoin, *Creative Director*; Conni Medina, M.A.Ed., *Editorial Director*; Jamey Acosta, *Associate Editor*; Neri Garcia, *Senior Designer*; Stephanie Reid, *Photo Researcher*; Rachelle Cracchiolo, M.A.Ed., *Publisher*

Image Credits

cover ts1/ZUMA Press/Newscom; p.1 ts1/ZUMA Press/Newscom; p.4 TSN Archives/Newscom; p.5 (left) ts1/ZUMA Press/Newscom, (right) Adrian Coroama/Shutterstock; p.6 Hutton Archive/Getty Images; p.7 Map Resources/Shutterstock; p.8 Library of Congress, LC-DIG-ppmsca-12888; p.9 Library of Congress, LOC_LC-USZC2-6201; p.10 Special Collections and University Archives, UO Libraries; p.11 ythac/Shutterstock; p.12 Collegiate Images/Getty Images; p.13 Associated Press; p.14 TSN Archives/Newscom; p.15 The Bridgeman Art Library/Getty Images; p.16 TSN/Icon SMI/Newscom; p.17 (top) Tim Bradley, (bottom) Associated Press; p.18 TSN Archives/Newscom; p.19 ts1/ZUMA Press/Newscom; p.20 Tim Bradley; p.21 Panworld Sports/Icon SMI/Newscom; p.22 ts1/ZUMA Press/Newscom; p.23 The Sporting News Archive/Newscom; p.24 TSN Archives/Newscom; p.25 TSN Archives/Newscom; p.26 Matt A. Brown/Icon SMI/Newscom; p.27 Cliff Welch/Icon SMI /Newscom; p.28 (left) TSN Archives/Newscom, (right) TSN/Icon SMI/Newscom; p.29 (left) The Sporting News Archive/Newscom, (right) TSN Archives/Newscom; p.32 Los Angeles Daily News/Newscom

Teacher Created Materials
5301 Oceanus Drive
Huntington Beach, CA 92649-1030
http://www.tcmpub.com

ISBN 978-1-4333-1597-8

Printed by: 590835
Printed in: China

Table of Contents

Meet Jackie

Jackie Robinson was a baseball player. He was also a **brave** man. He did things no one else had ever done. He stood up for what was right even though people were mean to him. He did this so everyone could play sports together.

Jackie and his teammates

African Americans and white baseball players could not play on the same teams until 1947.

Jackie in his baseball uniform

Young Jackie

Jackie was born in Georgia on January 31, 1919. Jackie's father left when he was six months old. His mother moved the family to California. She wanted a better life for her family.

Jackie and his family

Fun Fact

It is about 2,500 miles from Georgia to California. It took Jackie's family about 85 hours to make the trip by train. That is almost 4 days!

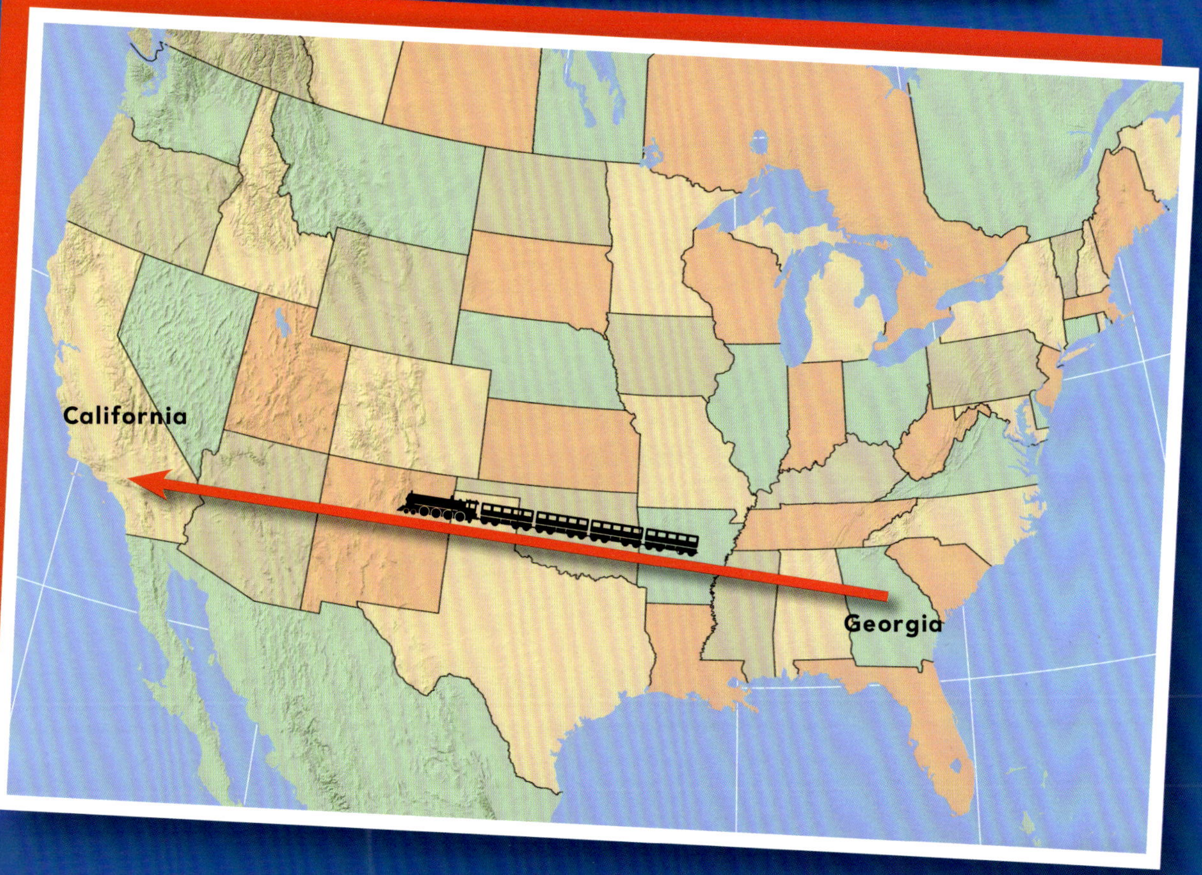

Back then, African Americans and white people were kept apart. This was called **segregation**.

African Americans could not sit with white people at movie theaters.

Life was hard for the Robinsons. African American neighborhoods (NAY-ber-hoods) were separated from white neighborhoods. Jackie's mother bought a house in a white neighborhood. The neighbors did not want the Robinsons to live there.

Theodore Roosevelt

Fun Fact

Jackie's full name was Jack Roosevelt Robinson. He was named after President Theodore Roosevelt.

The Robinson kids were good athletes. Jackie was the youngest. He had to play hard to keep up with his brothers and sisters. He was good at every sport he tried.

Mack Robinson

Fun Fact

Jackie's brother Mack earned a silver medal in track and field in the 1936 Olympics.

Sculptures of Mack and Jackie

Jackie worked hard to get into college. There, he played many sports. He broke records in basketball, football, and track. He was the first person to earn a varsity letter in four sports at his college.

Jackie playing basketball in college

Jackie playing football in college

Facing Unfairness

Jackie left college early. He went to fight in World War II. Jackie saw that African American soldiers were not treated the same as white soldiers. One day after Jackie came back from war, a bus driver told him to sit in the back of the bus. African Americans could not sit in the front of the bus with white people. Jackie **refused** to move to the back of the bus.

Jackie in his army uniform

Fun Fact

Rosa Parks also refused to move to the back of the bus. She did this eleven years after Jackie did.

Rosa Parks

At the time, African Americans were not allowed to play on sports teams with white players. Major League Baseball was open to white players only. Jackie played in the **Negro League**. He was one of the star players.

Jackie played for the Kansas City Monarchs.

Fun Fact

The Negro League was formed in 1897.

Jackie and his teammates in front of their bus

In 1945, Jackie met Branch Rickey. Branch ran the Brooklyn (BROOK-lin) Dodgers. He wanted African Americans to play baseball with white players. He asked Jackie to play Major League Baseball. He told Jackie that he would have to be brave. Jackie said yes.

Jackie signing his contract for the Dodgers

Fun Fact

Jackie had the best batting average in the league.

A Great Career

In 1947, many fans and players booed and called Jackie names. They did not want an African American to play baseball on a white team. But Jackie was a great player. He worked hard and played his best.

Baseball fans booing Jackie

Jackie playing first base

Fun Fact

Jackie had 29 stolen bases in 1947. That was the most!

Jackie steals home!

Jackie played first base for the Brooklyn Dodgers. He was a great hitter. He was good at stealing bases, too. He helped the team go to the World Series. Jackie was the first person ever to win the Rookie of the Year award!

Jackie receives the Rookie of the Year award for being the best new baseball player.

For the next 10 years, Jackie was one of the best players in baseball. He had a lifetime batting average of .311. In 1949, he won the Most Valuable Player award. He led the Brooklyn Dodgers to six **pennants**. They even won the World Series!

Dodgers win the 1952 National League pennant!

Fun Fact

Jackie was invited to play on the All-Star team six years in a row.

Jackie receives the Most Valuable Player award.

Paving the Way

Jackie was the first African American player in Major League Baseball. Being the first was not easy. But it changed the world. Today, players of all **races** play together. Jackie died on October 24, 1972. People today remember his talent and courage.

Players of all races together on one team

Fun Fact

Jackie made it into the Baseball Hall of Fame in 1962.

Time

1919

Jackie Robinson is born in Georgia.

1942–1944

Jackie serves in the U.S. Army.

1945

Jackie plays for the Kansas City Monarchs in the Negro League.

Line

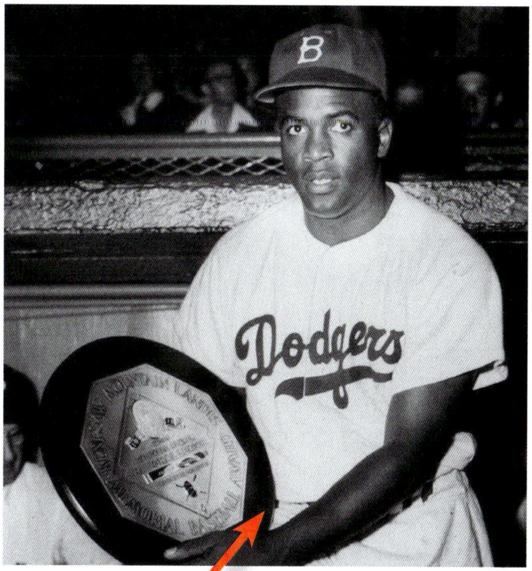

1947

Jackie is the first African American to play in the Major Leagues. He wins Rookie of the Year.

1949

Jackie wins the Most Valuable Player award.

1972

Jackie dies at the age of 53.

Glossary

African Americans—Americans whose families came from Africa

brave—not afraid

Negro League—a group of baseball teams with all African American players

pennants—flags used to symbolize championships

races—groups of people who have different skin color

refused—to say that you will not do something

segregation—the separation of people based on race or religion

Index

Americans Today

Jimmy Rollins is a baseball player. He was named the Most Valuable Player in 2007. He has stolen at least 20 bases every season. Jackie helped make his career possible.